A Twentieth Century Testimony

A Twentieth

Century Testimony

Malcolm Muggeridge

THOMAS NELSON
Nashville · Toronto · New York

introduction by
Thomas Howard

Library of Congress Cataloging in Publication Data

Muggeridge, Malcolm, 1903-
  A twentieth century testimony.
   1. Christian life—1960-   2. Muggeridge,
Malcolm, 1903-   I. Title.
BV4501.2.M74   248'.4   78-15925

U.S. ISBN 0-8407-5143-5
CANADIAN ISBN 0-17-600701-6

Good and evil provide the theme of the drama of our mortal existence. In this sense, they may be compared with the positive and negative points which generate an electric current. Transpose the points and the current fails, the lights go out, darkness falls, and all is confusion.

The darkness falling on our civilization is likewise due to a transposition of good and evil. In other words, what we are suffering from is not an energy crisis, nor an overpopulation crisis, nor a monetary crisis, nor a balance of payments crisis, nor an unemployment crisis—from none of these ills that are commonly pointed out—but from the loss of a sense of a moral order in the universe. Without that, no order whatsoever—economic, social, or political—is attainable.

For Christians, order is derived from that terrific moment, when, while all things were in quiet silence and that night was in the midst of her swift course, thine almighty Word leaped down from heaven out of thy royal throne, leaped down to dwell among us, full of grace and truth. It was thus that Christendom came into existence, and to abandon or repudiate the almighty Word from which it is derived would be infallibly to wind up two thousand years of history and ourselves with it.

—**Malcolm Muggeridge**

Introduction

It is always a piquant curiosity when a public figure converts to something. The Beatles seek out a guru; Cassius Clay becomes a Muslim; Sammy Davis Jr. converts to Judaism; an astronaut takes up Transcendental Meditation; T. S. Eliot declares himself an Anglo-Catholic; and so forth. People never know quite what to do. If the figure is magnetic enough, there may be a small momentary popular surge towards whatever the thing is. Or there may be an amused and hearty "Right on, man! You do your thing and we'll do ours." Or perhaps some knowing head-wagging: "Well, I could have told you this," or "Mmm . . . Poor duffer's gone soft in the head, you know."

The last, I think, is the general cultivated reaction to the spiritual odyssey of one of the most electrifying figures of our own time. He would not have been picked as a likely candidate for religious conversion, being not only an enormously civilized and urbane man of letters, but an **enfant terrible** of letters, a hard-headed journalist, a bodkin-tongued critic of the passing scene, and a general man-about-modern-affairs. ·

The man, of course, is Malcolm Muggeridge. A sometime journalist for British newspapers and editor of **Punch**, he is lately on British and American television, a personality who, everyone now knows, will regale and startle any audience with his wit, and will insist, with implacable iteration, that the modern world is busy abuilding, not the City of God, nor even the classless Eden of optimist liberalism, but, quite simply, Babel.

He may be another crazy and unclassifiable exhibit for the eyes of humanity, in the lineage of Ezekiel, John the Baptist, St. Simeon the Stylite, and St. Francis of Assisi. He may be a figure who, in his ferocious and single-minded separation from the spirit of his age and dedication to the task and message given him, appears as a warning and comfort to honest minds and as a dunce or a bore to fools.

The thing that sticks in everybody's craw is, of course, that the man has become a **Christian**. Here is all this urbanity and wit, and all this trove of knowledge amassed during several decades at the center of modern affairs—all this promise that we will now have a real elder prophet for our time who will help us with our agenda of dismantling history and superstition and of putting together a truly enlightened and liberal society. And what do we get? Doom. Jeremiads. Brickbats. **Jesus.**

For that is what the man is on about. Jesus. Of all the tiresome and dismaying backwaters for a modern eminence to dodge into, this, surely, is the most tiresome. Pulpy and rabbity minds have always fled from the hurly-burly and ambiguity of existence to the consolations of superstition. They have always chosen to placate the gods or hope for pie in the sky rather than to address themselves courageously and humbly to the hard, light-of-day realities of life. But that is for pulpy and rabbity minds. Here we have **Muggeridge** doing this. What ails the man?

If we want to find out what ails the man, we may do worse than to find out something about him. He gave us all a start (perhaps "start" in both its senses: a beginning, and a jolt) in his autobiography, the first two volumes of which appeared in 1973 and 1974 (**Chronicles of Wasted Time**, Wm. Morrow & Co.). In these chronicles he told of his Fabian Socialist upbringing, with the whole grey troupe of leftist votaries of the earthly (read Stalinist) paradise coming through his living room, either actually in the flesh, or in spirit, with Beatrice and Sidney Webb (whose niece Muggeridge had married). And he wrote of his years at Cambridge where, if we credit his wry portrait of himself as a feckless ne'er-do-well, we will conclude that his academic career was "scandalously desultory," to borrow the words he used elsewhere to describe Tolstoy's performance at school.

After university, he went to India as a teacher. His reflections on the British Raj (its suzerainty in India during the decades of Empire) are a bellwether of the sort of piercing and unsettling comment on the world scene he would be making for the rest of his life. One finds him poking pins into the balloon-like pretensions of pith-helmeted, be-braided British colonels and other pukka types, not, as one might confidently expect, by way of clearing the ground for a fierce tract on the virtues of self-government and the villainy of imperialism, but rather by way of letting the air out of **all** pretentiousness, imperial and local. In his descriptions of other British colonies, the wigged, plumed, and cockaded local chiefs who supplanted the moustachioed governors-general do not appear on stage as necessarily wiser and nobler men than their imperialist predecessors. Muggeridge is bemused by the whole odd phenomenon of man's struggle for power and glory. His reaction to the puffing and strutting of politicians, tycoons, and plenipotentiaries is not so much disgust as incredulity: What **can** they think they are about? Do they really believe it all? he seems to ask. This motif ran through his writings for decades before he was flagged down by the teachings of Jesus Christ and found divine corroboration for his own distrust of human vanity.

Most of Muggeridge's life was spent as a journalist. He was a foreign correspondent in Russia during the high and palmy days of Stalinist terror in the 1930s. He and his wife, like good English intellectuals and liberals, had gone to the Soviet Union as pilgrims with utopian stars in their eyes. Here now was the City of God come to earth, with the added advantage of having jettisoned God. The City of Man. The classless society. The dictatorship of the proletariat. The only difficulty in the enterprise was that it looked suspiciously like hell.

No one would see it, of course. Troops of rumpled humanitarian zealots from England and America made their pilgrimages and were shown the props and pasteboard sets of the Stalinist stage. They chose not to hear the shrieks coming from backstage, nor to see the NKVD hurrying half the population off to torture and the salt mines, nor to log the statistics of starvation following Stalin's gigantic collective agricultural plans. Once again, Muggeridge was bemused, more, if possible, by the murderously cynical gullibility and humbug of these Western observers than by the plain atrocities and banalities of the Soviet system. What he saw extinguished forever from his eyes the stars glimmering over any conceivable secular utopia. Monstrosity . . . tumescence . . . megalosaurian tyranny: clearly that's what you get from this sort of thing, he came to believe.

And once again we find in his writings, not the mere bitter fervor of the disenchanted partisan, but rather the more subtle and difficult awareness that **all** statecraft is shot through with this fearsome cupidity, vanity, and voraciousness, and that all of us exhibit it unless some great love or suffering has begun to purge it away. Long before he became enamored with such figures as Jesus, Augustine, St. Francis, Tolstoy, and Mother Teresa, Muggeridge seems to have avoided the mistake common to passionate moral conviction, that it is **those** guys (Stalin, or Hitler, or Roosevelt, or Nixon) who are the evildoers, and that **we** (our country, or our party, or our caucus, or, let's face it, **I**) were immaculately conceived. There is a wry awareness running all through his work of the unhappy irony that the thing that prevents most of us from being Attilas or Ivan the Terribles is not goodness so much as lack of the chance. But again, this does not make him the cynic. He winces, as it were, over the awareness that it is all true of himself first of all. Indeed, he makes the point that he has never come across any atrocity, any plunder, any outrage, or any perversion anywhere in history or society that he did not recognize as all too familiar; he had encountered it already in his own set of inclinations.

But this awareness does not poison his approach to others. That turns out to be vastly charitable. Not sentimental, but charitable.

Perhaps the salt that saves his mordant awareness of human fallibility from being morbid is humor. He cannot stop chuckling. His sheer zest for life, people, and words tumbles out all over. Appropriately, then, his career as a journalist was crowned with the editorship of **Punch**.

As it happens, I subscribed to **Punch** for the first time during Muggeridge's tenure as editor. It was part of a young man's effort to struggle out of the backwater he thought he was in and to leap into the main stream of civilized life. I subscribed to it along with the Manchester **Guardian** (the crinkly, tissue-paper, air-mail weekly edition), **The New Republic, The New Statesman,** and other pop highbrow journals. This was twenty years ago, and I remember in **Punch** the names of Claude Cockburn and Lord Altrincham as regular contributors. The note struck in the magazine was of sharp, urbane, agile mockery, the butt of it all ordinarily being the establishment pachyderm. Queen, Archbishop, Downing Street, tea—nothing was sacred. The cover was glossy with raffish, ersatz-child-art paintings of Punch and his dog in various poses and situations, instead of the dowdy filigree that had decked the cover for so long. It was very amusing and very remorseless.

Muggeridge himself looks back on that epoch with a certain wry demurral. (I am aware of the fact that I keep using the word "wry." It is necessary, the way the word "ice" would crop up more than once in a paper about Antarctica, or "savory" in a treatise on sauces. Wryness attends Muggeridge's outlook, and it bespeaks something important, it seems to me: There is a combination of amiability and self-deprecation and wit and seriousness of moral vision that yields a wry flavor to what he writes; and when we speak of what he writes, we speak of what he is, since his life has been words—millions and millions of them, as he says.)

In any event, he looks back on his **Punch** period with this certain demurral. He is struck by a sort of gruesome irony in it all—a sort of macabre poetic justice in the enterprise of trying to dredge up laughter from the slough of the modern West, especially from England in its decline. One of the things that seems now to strike him as grotesque about it is the pretentiousness and mendacity of a journalism like that, or indeed of any journalism. It is almost impossible to stay honest and clear-headed if you have to crank out either news or humor in enormous quantities for the maw of the public. The news, somewhere in there, becomes pure fantasy, creating bogus events out of nothing and then magnifying them into diurnal apocalypses in order to keep the populace tuning in and buying the sponsors' products if nothing else. And the humor becomes more and more abrasive and metallic until nothing at all is left behind but sophistication, ennui, and, eventually, inanity.

An obvious added irony here, of course, is that with all this distrust of journalism, Muggeridge was, and is, a journalist. He is also a prophet. But over the years his bread and butter has been journalism. It's all very well, we may protest, for Muggeridge to batter away at the pretensions of the news media, but then what on earth is he doing there (he is a frequent and popular guest on TV shows, for example)?

His position on this is no more anomalous, really, than that of a man crying out against gluttony, drunkenness, or debauchery. Presumably that man must eat and drink **something,** and, if he is married, may enjoy sex. He cannot take up a categorical position against the commodities of food, wine, and sex. Rather, he is decrying the brutalization that we bring on ourselves by deifying these commodities. By the same token, Muggeridge is not against communication, heaven knows. What appalls him is the spectacle of communication deified. Mass communication. Instant everything. The Juggernaut. The Demiurge. Implacable, omnipresent, omnipotent. Who will sound a note in behalf of doubt? In behalf, say, of sanity? He is willing to do so, although "sanity" as he sees it would be trivial and irrelevant to many of his colleagues and viewers, having to do, as it does, with such mouldy commodities as modesty and decency and purity and grace and charity and sanctity—all these inconsequential and embarrassing notions raked from the crannies of tradition and religion. They are certainly not gripping, newsworthy, or helpful in maintaining Nielsen ratings.

Anyone—pagan, Christian, or Jew—who has read anything that Muggeridge has written in the last decade and more, or who has seen him on television as a guest on someone else's program or narrating his own productions, knows well enough that he is obsessed with one topic, the way the prophets, apostles, and saints were obsessed with one topic. Goodness. Purity of heart. Truth. Sanity. Sanctity. God. Phrase it how we will, it comes to the same thing. He is **vox clamantis in deserto.** In the precincts of Vanity Fair, he is like the poet or sage or seer who stands on the hillside outside the city, calling out to the shopkeepers and holidaymakers, "That way lies madness and destruction!"

Sometimes people like this turn into bores—monomaniacal, garrulous, wild-eyed. But anyone who has ever met Muggeridge and his wife Kitty will have had any fears on this point dispelled. You spend most of your time, if you have the slightest love for words, in paroxysms of laughter. The repartee, the badinage, the sheer merriment darting and flashing through the air the whole time are like water from the fountain of

Helicon, a tonic to the soul. And one finds that what one has come upon in his writings is true of the man himself: razor-sharp wit, passionate moral conviction, unsentimental common sense, an appetite for sheer goodness, a noble capacity for disgust in the face of what is disgusting, and boundless mirth. But with this, nothing tawdry, nothing snide, nothing harsh or raucous or pettifogging or vulgar. All is clarity, agility, and charity.

When did he become a Christian? Who knows? For one thing, we need the third volume of his autobiography to bring his story up to date. But then Muggeridge himself might step around the question. When did I become a Christian? Well now, if you are asking for a date when I "decided for Christ," I'd prefer to say that I'm trying to decide for Christ all the way along now. It has not been so much a matter of one jump through a hoop as of beginning to follow in The Way, as the early Christians used to call it.

But I am putting words into his mouth. I can only guess, on the basis of having read everything I can get my hands on that he has written and of a few enormously happy visits with him. No one needs to speak for Muggeridge. When he is inadequate to tell his own story, the English language will have failed us all.

Thomas Howard
Hamilton, Massachusetts
May, 1978

A Twentieth Century Testimony

Dust to Dust...

England-
Whatlington, Sussex

When one is nearing the end of a life, as I am, my allotted span of three score years and ten already well passed, hair white and disappearing, breath short, eyes dim, grunting, coughing, groaning, with many other intimations of mortality in flesh and mind and spirit, it's natural enough to be thinking about death. This is particularly the case when I visit the graveyard where my father lies buried, with a space beside him which I expect to be occupying quite soon now. "Dust to dust," is how the burial service in the Book of Common Prayer puts it. Or, in my case, as I sometimes wonder, will the end be signalized by a celestial Voice on high proclaiming the single word "cut"?

From my earliest years I've been much given to thinking about death, some would think abnormally, or even morbidly so. First, I considered it as an infinitely remote and mysterious prospect; then, as the years passed, as an actual happening which must in due course befall me; and now as an event near-at-hand—so near that it quite cancels out all the plans and expectations and hopes relating to this world that have occupied my mind. As Dr. Johnson said of the man expecting to be hanged, "The prospect of death wonderfully concentrates the mind."

This might seem in contemporary terms a melancholy, if not unmentionable, case to be in—death having replaced sex as the great taboo, the dirty little secret. I, on the contrary, find it very uplifting, like the close of a June day—a distillation, as it were, of everything most beautiful and most loving in what has gone before. Death is a beginning, not an end. The darkness falls, and in the sky is a distant glow, the lights of St. Augustine's City of God. Looking towards them, I say over to myself John Donne's splendid words: **Death, thou shalt die.** In the graveyard, the dust settles; in the City of God, eternity begins.

**O that thou shouldst give dust a tongue
To cry to thee.**

So wrote George Herbert. A door of utterance for dust; words with a beginning and an end, expressing what never began and cannot end. Yet the passion to speak persists, like seeing someone off on a train, and, when the train begins to move, rushing along with it to get in one last word.

The true purpose of our existence,
to look for God . . .

England–
Robertsbridge, Sussex

For more than half a century I've been a communicator, what St. Augustine called a vendor of words. And the habit remains. My words have been tapped out on a typewriter or teleprinter, shouted down a telephone, mouthed from a platform, scribbled by hand, spoken into a microphone, recorded on tape or video. Words, words, words—millions and millions of them; particles of spray momentarily caught in the sunlight and then falling back into the ocean whence they came. Sonorous leading articles, trivial gossip paragraphs, pompous obituaries, news stories from our special correspondent—here, there, and everywhere; exhortation, speculation, every variety of composition. I have let loose a positive Niagara of words, frothing and churning on their tumultuous course.

When I look back on my life nowadays, which I sometimes do, what strikes me most forcibly about it is that what seemed at the time most significant and seductive, seems now most futile and absurd. For instance, success in all of its various guises; being known and being praised; ostensible pleasures, like acquiring money or seducing women, or travelling, going to and fro in the world and up and down in it like Satan, exploring and experiencing whatever Vanity Fair has to offer.

In retrospect all these exercises in self-gratification seem pure fantasy, what Pascal called "licking the earth." They are diversions designed to distract our attention from the true purpose of our existence in this world, which is, quite simply, to look for God, and, in looking, to find Him, and, having found Him, to love Him, thereby establishing a harmonious relationship with His purposes for His creation.

Contrary to what might be expected, I look back on experiences that at the time seemed especially desolating and painful with particular satisfaction. Indeed, I can say with complete truthfulness that everything I have learned in my seventy-five years in this world, everything that has truly enhanced and enlightened my existence, has been through affliction and not through happiness, whether pursued or attained. In other words, if it ever were to be possible to eliminate affliction from our earthly existence by means of some drug or other medical mumbo jumbo, as Aldous Huxley envisaged in **Brave New World,** the result would not be to make life delectable, but to make it too banal and trivial to be endurable. This, of course, is what the Cross signifies. And it is the Cross, more than anything else, that has called me inexorably to Christ.

I am a participant
in our Creator's purpose . . .

England –
The Countryside

It is often said that old age is a sort of second childhood. And it's true in a way. One does go back to childhood. For instance, I remember things that happened when I was a child much more clearly and vididly than things that have happened more recently. More often than not, yesterday is totally obliterated, but I can recall exactly happenings as long as fifty or sixty years ago. It is the same with places. With natural scenes, like a lovely field, the sheep, the orchard, the sky. Again it's like a child's sharp reaction, as though I were seeing a landscape for the first time, although, in fact, it is a familiar view.

And then with people, too. As a child one has the same sort of relationship with everyone; they are all uncles and aunts, brothers and sisters, belonging to one family, and so to be trusted, to be loved and to be confided in. Thus, when people see this second childhood as an intimation of senescence, I don't agree. I am more inclined to think of it as a conditioning process for eternity, as accustoming one to the circumstances that one is going to move into. Furthermore, it bears out those sayings of Jesus about how we have to be like a little child to understand His words and to enter His kingdom.

There is another thing that happens to me quite often nowadays. It sounds rather strange, but actually it is enormously delightful. I have a vivid sense of being half in and half out of my body, as though it were almost a tossup whether I am to go back fully into my body and resume my earthly life, or to make off and leave my battered old carcass behind me forever. In this curious state, in a sort of limbo between time and eternity, there are two convictions that I have, two very strong convictions. The first is of the incredible beauty of our earth and my fellow humans; of the earth's colors and shapes and smells and sounds, and of human love, and the delight of human work and human procreation, the continuance of life from generation to generation. All these things seem absolutely wonderful and beautiful. The second impression, stronger than I can possibly convey, is that as an infinitesimal particle of life, I am a participant in our Creator's purposes for His Creation, and that those purposes are loving and not malign, creative and not destructive, universal and not particular; and with that conviction comes a very great comfort and a very great joy.

Of course, in such a state of mind, one looks back on one's life, and all the worldly pursuits that it has involved, with a sort of distaste, as though it was all worthless—so much wasted time. On the other hand, I must admit that the profession of journalism, which I have practiced for the last half century and more, has one very great advantage: it gives one a very sharp sense indeed of the sheer buffoonery of power and of those who seek it and exercise it.

Without a god, men have to be gods themselves . . .

London –
Madame Trussaud's Exhibition

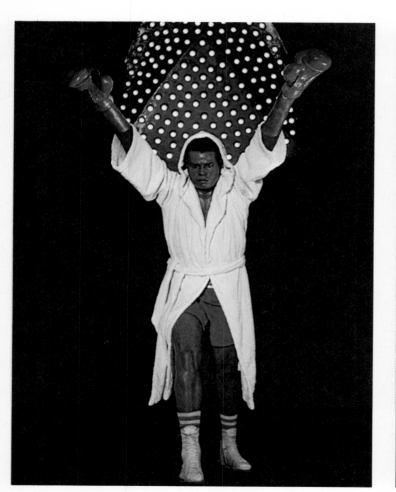

Without a god, men have to be gods themselves, and fabricate their own immortality, as they have in wax in London's Madame Tussaud's Exhibition, a place of images. In the beginning was the image, and the image became wax, and dwelt among us, full of absurdity. Here stand wax images of the famous and infamous dead, of the celebrated and notorious living. Above all are the gods and goddesses of the media—these, images of images, programmed at the punching of the tape recorder's button to shout and gesticulate in accordance with their pre-ordained roles. In this wax depository stands even an image of myself.

From time to time, I have a bizarre notion that I might change places with my wax image, and spend a few quiet days on Baker Street with Madame Tussaud's Figures, leaving my image to do the various things that I have got to do: to sit at my typewriter and grind out words; to hear the cry, "Action!" respond to it, and then relapse with the cry, "Cut." Or again when silence is prayed for by the toastmaster, to arise and state: "Your Grace, your Excellencies, my Lords, Ladies, and Gentlemen. . . ."

I like very much the notion of Pascal that people in authority need to dress up in order to justify their position of eminence. "If judges didn't wear ermine," Pascal said, "who could possibly suppose that they were capable of dispensing true justice?" We could say the same of priests in their vestments, scholars in their gowns, admirals in their gold braid and generals with their red tabs, kings and queens with their crowns and their orbs, and chefs with their tall white hats. In the same sort of way, clowns have to paint their faces in order that people may know they are being funny. Authority, in other words, requires an image. Men in relation to power become images; it is only in their relation to God that they dare to be men.

Here they all are, the captains and the kings, the great ones who ebb and flow with the moon. Kings and queens, presidents and politicians, soldiers and sailors, pontiffs and ideologues—all waxworks with their names written on water, or, in what amounts to the same thing in contemporary terms, written on a television screen; all stars in an interminable soap opera called history.

I've always had the feeling, from my very earliest memories, that somehow, somewhere, there was another dimension of reality where the fancy dress was put aside, the grease paint was washed off, the arc lights were lowered. Even as a child, if I happened to catch a glimpse of a local mayor in his regalia, or a local vicar in his, it filled me with a kind of wonder, as it might a child looking incredulously, unconvinced at a Father Christmas with a cotton wool beard.

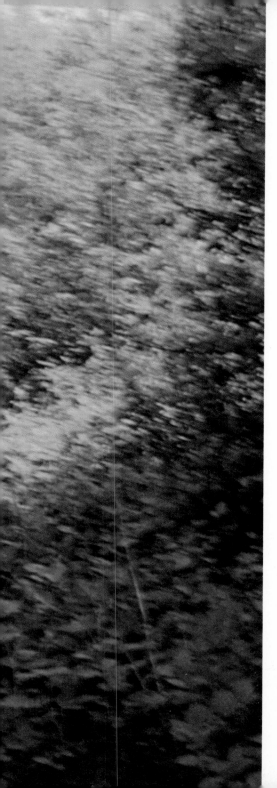

I feel as though all my life I've been looking for an alternative scene; for the face behind the cotton wool, the flesh beneath the wax, the light beyond the arc lights, time beyond the ticking of the clocks, a vista beyond the furthermost reach of mortal eyes even when magnified to thousands of light years, for a destiny beyond history. How extraordinary that I should have found it, not in flying up to the sun like Icarus, but in God coming down to me in the Incarnation.

**The Word became flesh
and dwelt among us . . .**

The Holy Land –
Galilee

A seeker after Reality (which means God) is bound sooner or later to be drawn to the Sea of Galilee, the scene of the Incarnation whereby God leaned down to become a Man—Jesus of Nazareth—in order that men might reach up and relate themselves to Him, their creator. Or, in the sublime imagery of the Fourth Gospel, whereby "the Word became flesh and dwelt among us full of grace and truth."

It has been my good fortune to visit Galilee on numerous occasions, in the way of my profession of communicator. Not long ago I was there again, almost certainly for the last time. I surveyed the scene with particular intensity, trying to store it in my mind, as one might study a beloved face never to be seen again.

Who can fail to be uplifted by the vista of Galilee? Other shrines and places of pilgrimage are liable to be fabricated, and are frequently vulgarized, but this one is somehow inviolate. Here are veritably the hills Jesus saw when He lifted up His eyes; this is the sea which provided His first disciples with their livelihood as fishermen, and which He often crossed, at times to avoid being in King Herod's jurisdiction. The same winds blow as in His time, the sun rises and sets in the same places. In the surrounding countryside many of His magical words were uttered, and the sick and disabled gathered in the hope of benefiting from His healing hand. It was from here that He took the road to Jerusalem, there to fulfill his inescapable destiny— the Crucifixion and the Resurrection that followed.

As one more poor pilgrim who has found his way belatedly to Galilee, a true child of his time with a sceptical mind and sensual disposition, let me then add my testimony to that of millions upon millions of others during the last twenty centuries. So, I say that the words Jesus spoke and the revelation He proclaimed were true when He spoke them, are true now, and will be true forever. Moreover, they provide for all who care to heed them a release from the fantasy of power, which is the world, transporting them into the reality of love, which is the kingdom not of this world that Jesus proclaimed. "Heaven and earth shall pass away," Jesus said, "but my words shall not pass away." We have them still, our most precious heritage. Here and now, those who care to live by and in them, while still living in our earthly city, can prepare themselves for the citizenship of the city of God which lies before them.

The promises Jesus made are still valid, and will continue so to be. Particularly true is His promise that He would not disappear from the world after His death, but continue to be accessible to those who sought Him. "Lo, I am with you always," He said to His disciples, "Even unto the end of the world." So it follows that in the afflictions of this world, no one needs ever lack a comforter; in the hardships of this world, no one needs ever lack a helper; in the stumblings and losing of one's way, which are inevitable in this world, no one needs ever lack an arm to lean on, a guide to show the way.

Yet still there is something else; something that, searching my heart, I find very difficult to express in words. . . . Accept the everlasting truth of Jesus' revelation, accept the everlasting validity of the promises He made. But still there is something else, an extraordinary illumination that comes flooding in on one's being, an extraordinary awareness of quite exceptional poignancy and force; a knowledge past knowing, a hope past hoping. Call it **faith,** which swallows up all the little intricacies of doubt and factual fidgeting. Call it being **reborn,** a new creature arising out of the dust and grubbiness of worldly living, like a butterfly out of its chrysalis. Whatever it may be called, it came to pass in Galilee. A new dimension was added to our mortal existence; a new freedom, not for a tiny elite, not based on institutions or propositions, but burgeoning in each human heart and needing only to be allowed to grow.

this wilderness is suddenly
full of joy and hope . . .

The Holy Land –
The Wilderness

After his baptism in the waters of the River Jordan by John the Baptist, our Lord made for the wilderness—probably this very one lying between Jerusalem and Jericho. The apostle Paul did the same thing after his Damascus Road experience. So have countless others, from hermits subsisting in remote and inaccessible caves—many such in this neighborhood—to troubled souls to be seen in the early morning walking in city parks and beside ornamental waters before the day's noises and movements have begun.

What the wilderness offers is its emptiness and barrenness . . . and silence. Not a tree or a street, not a building, not a telegraph pole, not a road or a vehicle in sight. Nothing to suggest human habitation, apart from an occasional flock of skinny sheep and goats, or vultures flying through the sky.

So, in the wilderness, the world seems far away. No social life, no media, no occasion for bitterness or frustration. Just an arid haven of refuge, a dusty paradise. No votes to cast, women to seduce, money to accumulate, celebrity to acquire. All the habitual pursuits of the ego and the appetites are suspended.

I love the wilderness because, when all these pursuits of mind and body have been shed, what remains—insofar as this is attainable in our mortal condition—is an unencumbered soul, with no other concern than to look for God. And looking is finding. And finding, one may dare to hope, is keeping. This is what St. Francis of Assisi meant when he spoke of being naked on the naked earth; this is the most sublime state a human being can aspire to: being in the wilderness alone with God.

From such an encounter with God, what emerges? That we are indeed made in His image, and, though fallen creatures and inheritors of Adam's curse, we may aspire to participate in His purposes. What those purposes are we cannot know, what they portend we cannot imagine. Nevertheless, knowing God brings with it the requisite faith to surrender wholly to His purposes. Then at last we can pray, really meaning it, fully accepting its implications, that line in the Lord's Prayer—**Thy will be done**—which is all there is to say to God, then or at any time.

When we surrender our will to God, the wilderness is suddenly full of joy and hope; it does veritably blossom like a rose, in the confident knowledge that nothing can befall us to our ultimate hurt other than to become separated from God. All other ills than this are transitory, and, like clouds melting away in the sun's glow, come to be incorporated in the radiance of God's universal love. Nor need we belabor the skies with cries to Him, since we have at hand a mediator in one who also came to this wilderness—the living Christ.

It must be said that at this moment in history, dark clouds are gathering everywhere, especially in the Middle East where so many battles have been fought, so many empires have risen and fallen. The Middle East still seems to be a focus of the world's tension. There are so many intimations that men are increasingly turning away from God and believing in their own self-sufficiency, thinking that **they** can decide who should live and who should be put down, what babies should be born and which should be destroyed in the womb before they even come into this world, intruding into our very genes to resort and rearrange them with a view to creating human beings according to their preferences.

Yet even if this nightmare should come to pass, and it might, but I doubt it, I feel sure that in some remote jungle, a forgotten naked savage would daub a stone with colored mud and prostrate himself before it, in that act ensuring that yet another chapter will open in the never ending drama of man's relationship to his Creator. It would also ensure that men looking for inspiration and illumination will turn not to their laboratories and their computers, but to the wilderness and their Creator.